MW00610012

Lee Bul live forever Act Two

cover, this page and following
14 pages:
Lee Bul, *Live Forever I*, 2001
fiberglass with acoustic foam, black
leather upholstery, plexiglass and
electronic equipment
100 x 60 x 38 inches
Produced in collaboration with
The Fabric Workshop and Museum
Photos: Aaron Igler

san francisco art institute
4·6·2001 – 5·19·2001

the fabric workshop and museum
11·9·2001 – 1·5·2002

orange county museum of art
1·26·2002 – 4·28·2002

new museum of contemporary art
5·17·2002 – 7·7·2002

the power plant
12·7·2002 – 3·2·2003

the scottsdale museum of contemporary art
5·10·2003 – 8·17·2003

henry art gallery
10·12·2003 – 1·14·2004

Introduction marion boulton stroud
Insidious Pop ellen bethany napier
Exhibition Checklist
Selected Exhibition History
Bibliography

PUBLISHED AS A COOPERATIVE PROJECT DEVELOPED BY THE FABRIC WORKSHOP
AND MUSEUM, PHILADELPHIA, AND THE SAN FRANCISCO ART INSTITUTE

ISBN 0-9619760-8-X

INTRODUCTION by Marion Boulton Stroud

Lee Bul's project *Live Forever* marks the second successful collaborative exhibition and residency between two institutions, The Fabric Workshop and Museum, Philadelphia, and the San Francisco Art Institute. The first was with French artist Marie-Ange Guilleminot, whose captivating sculptural project, *Sea Urchin*, graced both our galleries in 2000. Part sculpture, part garment, *Sea Urchin* was made from Tyvek, and in the hands of the artist transformed from chair, to cape, to tent, to parachute with an ingenious, yet deceptively simple, system of rope pulls. Our photographer and videographer Aaron Igler captured Marie-Ange Guilleminot's and Lee Bul's projects on film at both institutions, and many of those photographs are featured in this book. The Fabric Workshop and Museum and the San Francisco Art Institute collaborated on many aspects of each artist's residency, contributing the best resources that each had to offer to the creation and exhibition of these extraordinary new works of art.

Live Forever is Lee Bul's latest futuristic intervention into contemporary culture. Energetic, multi-dimensional, and highly entertaining, the project is not only a sight to see, but perhaps more importantly, it is an experience to have and remember. When the artist first visited The Fabric Workshop and Museum in the winter of 2000, she brought scenes from the movie *2001: A Space Odyssey*, and described her vision for a series of space capsules. As she contemplated the idea of time travel, her first idea for an egg-shaped capsule eventually metamorphosed into a fascinating race car-like form, which became known as "the pod." Over the course of the next year, these pod forms became reality, and eventually their interiors were upholstered with brilliant orange, jet black, and powder blue leather, and equipped with audio and video karaoke systems.

As an art installation, *Live Forever* asks of its viewers only that they indulge themselves by slipping into one of the luxuriously outfitted pods and singing along to a popular song of their choosing from a song list provided by the artist. As in traditional karaoke, still a sweeping phenomenon of contemporary Asian culture, Lee Bul's pods provide the lyrics so participants can sing along confidently—though in this case, it is in the privacy and comfort of a futuristic race car. While a participant sings inside the pod, the changing imagery on three large-scale video projections reveals the song chosen by the individual.

Live Forever is part science fiction, part pop culture. These space age cars practically take off into space when you first encounter them in a darkened and dramatically lit exhibition room. Lee Bul is a futuristic dreamer, and her increasingly powerful projects make her a pillar of art at the turn of the century.

Ambitious work such as *Live Forever* rarely results from the efforts of just one person. In this case, the artist worked closely with two institutions in the United States to realize different aspects of the piece—and this international collaboration was no small accomplishment given the enormous distance between Seoul, San Francisco, and Philadelphia. Project director Helen Cahng of The Fabric Workshop and Museum focused her considerable talents on overseeing the creative evolution of the pods and their installation in Philadelphia. Gheorghe Adam, a veritable genius as a sculptor and technical fabricator, labored for nearly a year to create the pods in Styrofoam before undertaking the highly difficult process of casting fiberglass for each pod's final form. Aaron Igler, photographer, and Matthew Suib, videographer, came up with creative solutions to resolve the many electronic design and technical issues for the karaoke pods, and construction technician Doina Adam contributed her problem-solving skills to make the interiors of the pods beautiful and functional. In San Francisco, Bul worked with students from the Art Institute to film new video for the piece.

Additionally, Ellen Napier, Associate Director of The Fabric Workshop and Museum, worked tirelessly to manage the many logistical aspects of the collaboration, as did Karen Moss, Director of Exhibitions and Public Programs at the San Francisco Art Institute. Clara Kim curated the San Francisco portion of the exhibition, and generously served as translator for Lee Bul's public lecture in Philadelphia in November, 2001. Their collective efforts also resulted in an ambitious North American tour schedule for *Live Forever*. We are pleased to thank Elizabeth Armstrong and Irene Hoffman at the Orange County Museum of Art, Lisa Phillips and Dan Cameron at the New Museum of Contemporary Art, Wayne Baerwaldt and Xandra Eden at the Power Plant, Susan Krane at the Scottsdale Museum of Contemporary Art, and Elizabeth Brown at the Henry Art Gallery, for their participation in the exhibition tour.

For the production of this catalogue, we owe our gratitude to Conny Purtill, designer, and Kelly Mitchell, consulting editor. Charged with the difficult task of conveying in two dimensions the many surfaces, textures and viewpoints within this multimedia installation, Conny developed a dynamic and vibrant design for both volumes of this publication. Kelly Mitchell applied her great talents to ensuring that the disparate pieces of information came together in a cohesive, coherent whole. We thank them both for their patience, flexibility, and dedication. In addition, we are grateful to photographer Gene Mopsik for his enormous efforts in documenting the project from the construction of the pods through to the opening celebrations.

Janet Samuel, registrar of The Fabric Workshop and Museum, and Ursula Ahrens, assistant registrar, are ably organizing the many aspects of shipping for the exhibition tour of *Live Forever*. With great ingenuity, Paul Swenbeck and Joy Feasley, art handlers for The Fabric Workshop and Museum, managed to move and transport these very large pods into places they were never intended to fit.

Lee Bul's colleague, Kyung-mee Park, contributed greatly to resolving many decisions along the way, and we thank her for her involvement.

It gives me great pleasure to thank Ella King Torrey, President of the San Francisco Art Institute, whose talent, leadership and vision guided this project from beginning to end. She oversaw every aspect, large and small, of the project's development, and pulled everyone together from all corners of the earth. I thank her from the bottom of my heart, and look forward to continuing our bi-coastal relationship with more projects in the future.

Finally, to Lee Bul we offer our most heartfelt appreciation. It is her creativity and faith in this collaboration that deserves our greatest admiration and our greatest thanks.

iNsidious pop by Ellen Bethany Napier

Live Forever brings together a breadth of ideas that Lee Bul has explored for over a decade. Through five series of work—*Cyborgs and Monsters, Interventions, Majestic Splendor, Monuments,* and the Karaoke projects—as well as many discrete sculptures, Lee has embarked on an ambitious and sophisticated investigation into experiences of popular culture, death and decay, art histories and traditions, technology and entertainment. In *Live Forever*, these themes are synthesized into an original installation that is activated by its audience. The range of media incorporated into this new project—video, sculpture, sound, drawing, performance, and computer-aided design— have also long been part of the artist's practice.

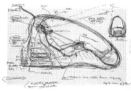

The complete project *Live Forever* consists of three fully functional karaoke pods and three original videos. In this exhibition, these works are accompanied by a series of process materials, including drawings, sketches, computer-aided designs, and a full–scale pink foam prototype for the pod from which the original casts were taken. The media and themes for each element of this new exhibition relate to the artist's larger body of work; viewing the two together serves to illuminate the depth and acuity of Lee's interests and vision.

The inclusion of Lee Bul's drawings and computer-aided designs show the evolution of the artist's karaoke projects, beginning with *Gravity Greater than Velocity*, originally exhibited in the Korean Pavilion at the Venice Biennale in 1999. In this presentation two upright booths, made from polycarbonate and lined with velvet, were accompanied by the video *Amateurs*. Lee went on to further explore the possibilities of presentation, experimenting with the placement of the viewer in relation to the audience. In 2000, at the Shanghai Biennial, Lee exhibited *Anthem*, in which the viewer stood on a high platform and looked out over the video. Without a booth, viewers were fully visible as they performed. With *Anthem*'s rapidly-moving images of urban streets, the artist's interest in speed and the passage of time, and the related idea of travel (in both space and time) begin to find a physical presence in the work. In *Live Forever*, Lee's third video and karaoke project, a new karaoke capsule evolved. The original sketches show that initially, the artist envisioned a capsule made from a translucent material, so that a person inside the pod would be somewhat visible to those on the outside. Handcrafted from fiberglass and plexiglass, the final capsules take the form of some sort of futuristic vehicle, capable of an all-new mode of transportation.

Gravity Greater than Velocity, 1999
polycarbonate panels on steel frame, velour, sponge, karaoke equipment, LCD monitor
98 1/2 x 72 1/2 x 47 1/4 inches
Photo: Rhee Jae-yong

conceptual sketch for the production of karaoke pod, 2000

live forever ii + amateurs

The first of the three pods is lined with orange leather. Stepping into the pod, the viewer dons headphones, and pulls the door down to close him/herself into the small, upholstered interior space. A small LCD screen inside the pod plays the video *Amateurs* as a background while the lyrics scroll by. After grabbing the microphone and selecting a song from the list, the performance begins. The pod is relatively soundproof, but that does not fully assuage a participant's initial unease and the sense of being observed. The windows in the sides of the pod expose the occupant to the outside world, and vice versa. And although the music is not played in the open gallery space, the words to the chosen song also appear in the larger-than-life video projection on the opposite wall, available for all to see.

Why this discomfort? If a performance is something one does for an audience, why the desire for privacy? Why perform for oneself? What is happening when one sings in front of a mirror alone? Lee brings to light the performance as a complex social act, and provides a situation in which the simple act of picking up a microphone alters a complicated public and private construct. The urge to be seen and

the wish to hide are connected in this experience. And while these notions may be understood at the far end of the spectrum—where many of the greatest performers are those who most need to hide themselves—this premise becomes more difficult to assimilate at a personal level. Like the teenage girls who inhabit the accompanying video, one may discover a strange territory of not wanting to be looked at, but wanting to be seen.

Closing oneself inside the capsule offers a certain degree of privacy. It is, however, a complicated and ambivalent refuge, which (like most forms of protection) can quickly become claustrophobic and suffocating. Many have noted the similarity of the pod to a coffin. This maleficent protection is an ongoing theme in Lee's work, and relates very directly to her continuing *Cyborgs and Monsters* series. Using materials such as silicone or porcelain, Lee has created a number of sculptural hybrid creatures with a combination of organic (arms, tentacles, breasts and wings) and mechanical forms. These figures are partly alien, partly familiar, and often obviously incomplete. Like the pods, the pristine elegance of the exterior shell belies the complex and ambiguous relationship of the constituent parts or the internal experience. And like the *Cyborgs*, the pod experience continues the artist's investigation of the protection and also the loss—even death—that occurs when one asks technology to mediate for the body.

live forever iii + anthem

The second pod—identical to the first, except that it is lined with silver–blue leather—is accompanied by the video *Anthem*, which, like *Amateurs*, is projected both inside and outside of the pod. *Anthem* features images of a city—of urban life, popular culture, and public spaces, all at an alarming speed. Shaped like a vehicle, and accompanied by a popular soundtrack, the capsule provides all of the necessary trappings for a journey. The futuristic shape of the capsule and the nostalgia invoked by the music make it completely unclear whether this road trip takes one forward or backward. What ensues is a bit of both: a ranging journey through time, space, and culture.

Time—whether accelerated, suspended or forgotten—is also a concept the artist has explored in previous work. In a series of performances or *Interventions*, the artist infiltrated public spaces such as the Kimpo airport and the streets of downtown Tokyo wearing soft sculptural costumes (she even tried to board a plane, but the costume was too large for a single seat). Adorned with strange orifices and appendages, the artist interrupted, stopped, and ultimately altered the real–time experience of urban life. In another series of work, *Majestic Splendor*, Lee allowed time to naturally take its course. Exhibited in 1997 at the Museum of Modern Art in New York, the installation was comprised of 200 mylar bags, each containing a dead fish decorated with sequins. Immediately, the fish began to decompose. Although the gallery was perfumed, after three days, the smell became oppressive. With each passing hour and each passing day, the fish continued to decay, giving the passage of time a physical and tangible presence.

Amaryllis, 1999
hand-cut polyurethane panels on aluminum armature, enamel coating
82 5/8 x 47 1/4 x 70 7/8 inches
Photo: Rhee Jae-yong

Sorry for Suffering—You Think I'm a Puppy on a Picnic?, 1990
12-day performance, Kimpo Airport, Narita Airport, downtown Tokyo, Dokiwaza Theater, Tokyo

Majestic Splendor (detail), 1991
fish, sequins, plastic bag
7 x 6 inches
Photo: Joo Myung-duk

live forever i

Lined with black leather, the third pod is accompanied by Lee's most recent video, *Live Forever*. Created during the artist's residency at the San Francisco Art Institute and filmed in the Tonga Room of the historic Fairmont Hotel, this video is actually created from still slides, morphed into motion using a computer. The hotel bar acts as a symbol for many of the issues that make up the layers of *Live Forever*: transience and travel, entertainment, and the complex human experience when something temporary stands in for something permanent.

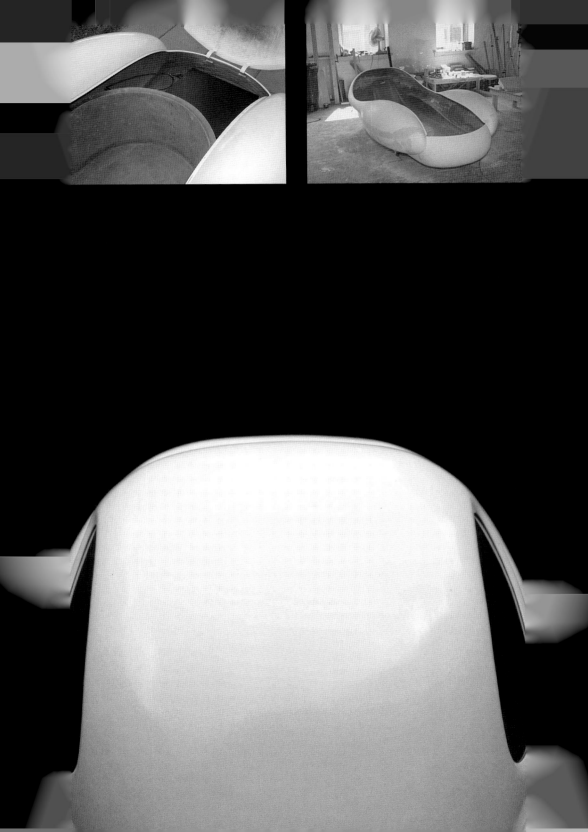

The latter of these ideas is also at work in Lee's *Monuments*, a series of enormous inflatable structures each with a printed image of a woman. Like the fish in *Majestic Splendor*, the female depicted on each monument is adorned with accessories, which read as iconographies for the feminine (lilies, beads, feathers, dolls). And like her performance costumes, many *Monuments* have various soft sculptural appendages. Using the language and materials of advertising and entertainment, Lee employs vinyl and air pumps for her contemporary version of a type of sculpture traditionally defined as being lasting and weighty. Presented in exterior and interior locations, these monuments are playful and fresh, but also empty and hollow in response to a fading sense of history and tradition.

It is not just the forms, but also the subjects of such monuments that interest Lee Bul. Pop stars today often act as heroes, although the protection they offer is in the form of escape. Movies such as Martin Scorcese's *King of Comedy*, or the more recent *Nurse Betty* have charted the pitfalls and pleasures available through contact with popular media. But through *Live Forever*, one can experience on a more personal level both the insidiousness and the fun of pop music, with all of its infectious melodies.

Unlike so much recent spectacle-oriented art, something darker lurks beneath the surface of *Live Forever*, and the pleasures it offers leave a lasting unease. The pods are indeed amazingly fun, yet there is a lingering melancholy and ambivalence to the very personal experience they offer. Questions about our public and private selves, the body and its relation to technology, movement through time, loss, tradition, entertainment, protection, sickness, and fun; all come together in three portable capsules. In *Live Forever*, Lee creates an environment in which it is only somewhat safe to enjoy the ride.

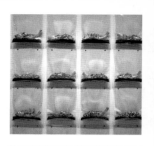

Majestic Splendor, 1997
partial view of installation, MoMA, NY
fish, sequins, potassium permanganate, mylar bags
141 3/4 x 161 3/8 inches
Photo: Robert Puglisi

Hydra II (Monument), 1999
photo print on vinyl, air pumps
472 1/2 x 275 5/8 x 236 1/4 inches
Photo: Yasunori Tanioka
Courtesy: Nanjo & Associates

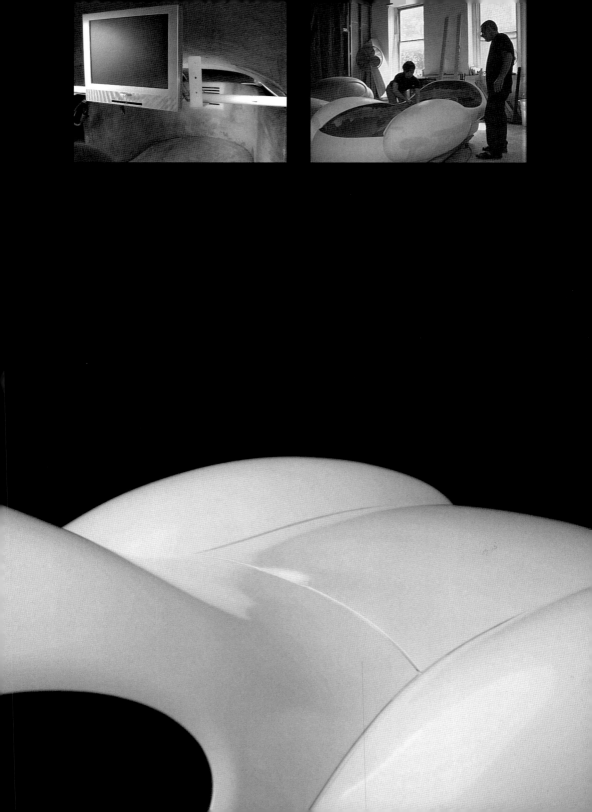

exhibition checklist

1 *Live Forever I*, 2001
fiberglass with acoustic foam, plexiglass, black leather upholstery, electronic equipment and three audio compact discs
100 x 60 x 38 inches
PRODUCED IN COLLABORATION WITH THE FABRIC WORKSHOP
AND MUSEUM, PHILADELPHIA

2 *Live Forever II*, 2001
fiberglass with acoustic foam, plexiglass, orange
leather upholstery, electronic equipment and one
audio compact disc
100 x 60 x 38 inches
PRODUCED IN COLLABORATION WITH THE FABRIC WORKSHOP
AND MUSEUM, PHILADELPHIA

3 *Live Forever III*, 2001
fiberglass with acoustic foam, plexiglass, silver-blue
leather upholstery, electronic equipment and one
audio compact disc
100 x 60 x 38 inches
PRODUCED IN COLLABORATION WITH THE FABRIC WORKSHOP
AND MUSEUM, PHILADELPHIA

4 *Live Forever Prototype*, 2001
styrofoam
100 x 60 x 38 inches
PRODUCED IN COLLABORATION WITH THE FABRIC WORKSHOP
AND MUSEUM, PHILADELPHIA

5 *Amateurs*, 1999
video on DVD; shown inside *Live Forever II* and as a single
channel video projection

6 *Anthem*, 2000
video on DVD; shown inside *Live Forever III* and as a single
channel video projection

7 *Live Forever*, 2001
video on DVD; shown inside *Live Forever I* and
as a single channel video projection
PRODUCED IN COLLABORATION WITH THE SAN FRANCISCO ART
INSTITUTE

8 Six Untitled Drawings for *Gravity Greater Than
Velocity*, 2000
ink, graphite, marker, and/or wash on graph paper
or white paper
8 ¹/₂ x 11 inches to 11 x 17 inches each

9 Three Untitled Drawings for *Anthem*, 2000
ink on notebook paper or white paper
8 ¹/₂ x 11 each

10 Thirteen Untitled Drawings for *Live Forever*,
2000–2001
ink, marker, paint, wash, and/or graphite on graph paper
or white paper
7 x 10 inches to 11 x 17 inches each

11 Nine Untitled Computer–Aided Designs for
Live Forever, 2000
computer prints on paper
8 ¹/₂ x 11 inches each

All works appear courtesy the artist and PKM Projects, Seoul

selected exhibition history

Born Yongwol, South Korea 1964
Studied Sculpture at Hong-Ik University, Seoul
Lives and works in Seoul

solo exhibitions

2002
The Fabric Workshop and Museum, Philadelphia,
and San Francisco Art Institute, San Francisco
(traveled to Orange County Museum of Art,
Newport Beach, CA; New Museum of Contemporary
Art, New York; The Power Plant, Toronto; The
Scottsdale Museum of Contemporary Art, Arizona;
and the Henry Art Gallery, Seattle)
Le Consortium centre d'art contemporain, Dijon

Museé d'art Contemporain, Marseille

Rodin Gallery, Samsung Museum, Seoul

pkm gallery, Seoul

2001
SCAI the Bathhouse, Tokyo

BAWAG Foundation, Vienna

2000
Kukje Gallery, Seoul

Fukuoka Asian Art Museum, Fukuoka, Japan

1999
Kunsthalle, Bern

Korean Pavillion, Venice Biennale, Venice

1998
Artsonje Center, Seoul

1997
Museum of Modern Art, New York

1994
A Space, Toronto

1988
IL Gallery, Seoul

selected group exhibitions

2002
The Uncanny: Experiments in Cyborg Culture,
Vancouver Art Gallery, Vancouver

2001
Record All Over, 9th Biennale de l'image en mouve-
ment, Musée d'art moderne et contemporain, Geneva

ARS 01: Third Space, Kiasma Museum of
Contemporary Art, Helsinki

Egofugal, 7th International Istanbul Biennial

Connivence, 6th Biennale de Lyon

Preview exhibition, Kanazawa Contemporary
Art Museum, Japan

Body as Byte, Neues Kunstmuseum Luzern, Lucerne

01.01.01: Art in Technological Times, San Francisco
Museum of Modern Art, San Francisco

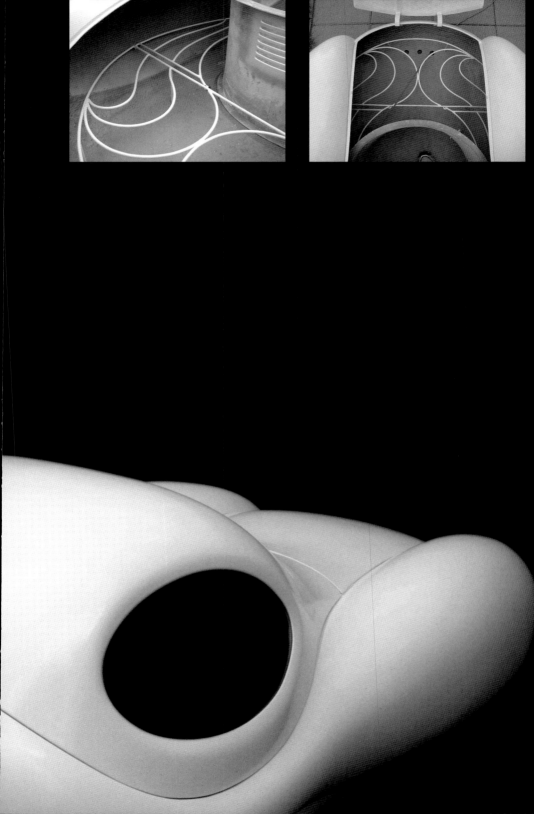

selected group exhibitions CONTINUED

My Reality: The Culture of Anime, Des Moines Art Center, Des Moines (traveled to Brooklyn Art Museum, New York and Contemporary Arts Center, Cincinnati)

2000

Shanghai Biennial, Shanghai Art Museum, Shanghai

media_city seoul, Seoul Metropolitan Art Museum, Seoul

Echigo–Tsumari Art Triennial, Echigo-Tsumari, Japan

Continuum 001, Centre for Contemporary Art, Glasgow

Let's Entertain, Walker Art Center, Minneapolis (traveled to Centre Georges Pompidou, Paris; Portland Art Museum, Portland, Oregon; Kunstmuseum Wolfsburg, Wolfsburg, Germany; and Miami Art Museum, Miami)

1999

dAPERTutto, 48th Venice Biennale, Venice

Zeitwenden, Kunstmuseum, Bonn (traveled to Kunstlerhaus Wien and Museum Moderner Kunst Stiftung Ludwig, Vienna)

1998

Hugo Boss Prize Exhibition, Guggenheim Museum SoHo, New York

The Natural World. Vancouver Art Gallery, Vancouver

1997

Cities on the Move, Wiener Secession, Vienna (traveled to capc Musée d'art contemporain, Bordeaux; P.S.1, New York; Kiasma Museum of Contemporary Art, Helsinki; Louisiana Museum of Modern Art, Humblebaek, Denmark; and Hayward Gallery, London)

Fast Forward, The Power Plant, Toronto

L'autre, 4th Biennale de Lyon

1995

Information and Reality, Fruitmarket Gallery, Edinburgh

Korean Contemporary Art Today, 1st Kwangju Biennial, Kwangju, Korea

New Asian Art, Japan Foundation Forum, Tokyo

1993

1st Asia Pacific Triennial, Queensland Art Gallery, Brisbane, Australia

1991

Interaction, Five-day performance at Suwon Castle, Suwon, Korea

1990

Song of the Fish, Performance, Dong Soong Art Center, Seoul

Sorry for Suffering—You Think I'm a Puppy on a Picnic?, Twelve day performance beginning in Kimpo Airport, Korea and continuing throughout various sites in Tokyo

bibliography
books and catalogues

Erlebte Modelle/Model Experience.
Kurzmeyer, Roman. Vienna and New York: Springer Verlag, 2000.

Hugo Boss Prize 1998.
New York, Guggenheim Museum, 1998.

Lee Bul.
Ahn, Soyeon. Seoul: Samsung Museum of Modern Art, 2002.

Lee Bul.
Kim, Sun-jung, and Hans Ulrich-Obrist. Seoul. Artsonje Center, 1998.

Lee Bul: In Medias Res
Kim, Won-bang, et al. Seoul: Ssamzie Art Book, 1999.

Lee Bul: The Divine Shell.
Vienna: BAWAG Foundation, 2001.

Lee Bul: Monster + Cyborg.
Fukuoka: Fukuoka Asian Art Museum, 2000.

Let's Entertain: Life's Guilty Pleasures.
Vergne, Philippe, et al. Minneapolis, Walker Art Center, 2000.

London, Barbara. "Lee Bul," in *La Biennale de Venezia 48a Esposizione Internazionale d'Arte dAPERTutto.*
Szeeman, Harald and Lavelli, Liveriero (eds.). Venice: Edizioni la Biennale de Venezi/Marsilio, 1999.

Szeeman, Harald. "Lee Bul," in *4e biennale de lyon d'art contemporain: l'autre.*
Réunion des Musées Nationaux, 1997.

The Uncanny: Experiments in Cyborg Culture.
Grenville, Bruce, et al. Vancouver: Vancouver Art Gallery and Arsenal Pulp Press, 2001.

periodicals

Farquharson, Alex. "Lee Bul at Artsonje Center."
Frieze, issue 45 (March/April 1999): 83–4.

Fouser, Robert. "Lee Bul."
Art AsiaPacific, no. 28 (Fall 2000): 54–61.

Gautherot, Franck. "Supernova in Karaoke Land."
Flash Art, vol. 34, no. 217 (March/April 2001): 80–3 + cover.

Helfand, Glen. "Sing a Song."
Artbyte, vol. 4, no. 2 (July/August 2001): 66–7.

Lee, Bul. "Obsessions."
Art Journal, vol. 59, no. 3 (Fall 2000): 105–7.

Lee, James B. "Stealth and Sensibility."
ARTnews, vol. 94, no. 4 (April 1995): 128–9.

Volkart, Yvonne. "Lee Bul."
make, issue 89 (September/November 2000): 4–7.

Volkart, Yvonne. "Lee Bul, Kunsthalle Bern."
Flash Art, vol. 32, no. 206 (May/June 1999): 121–2.

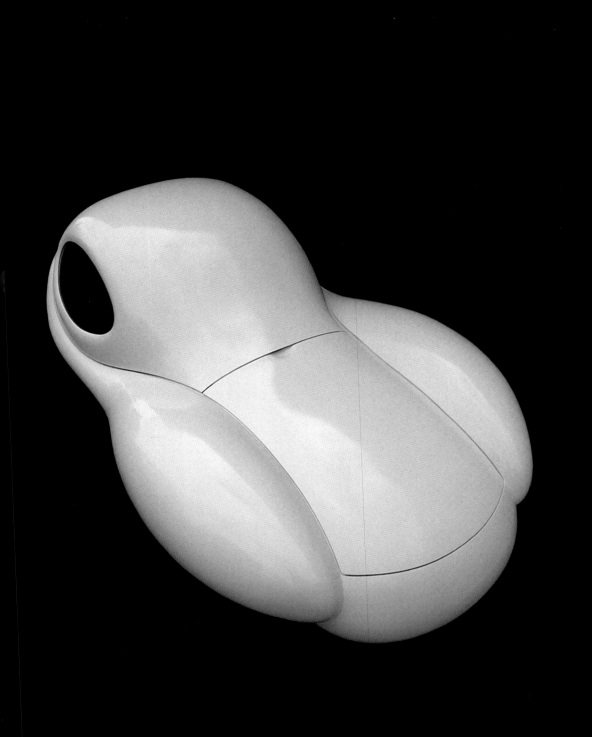

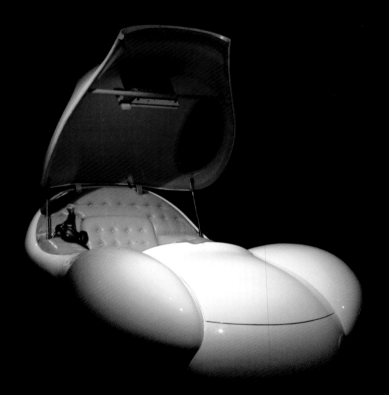

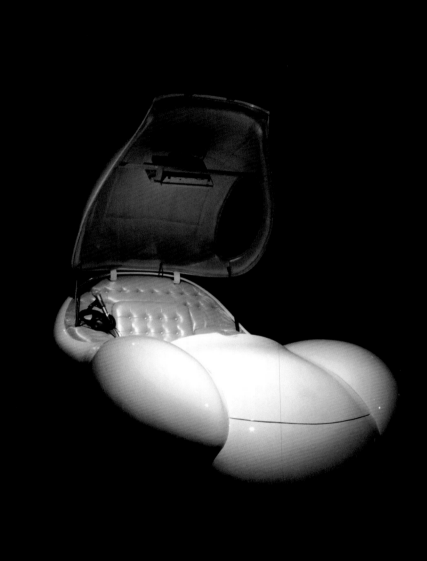

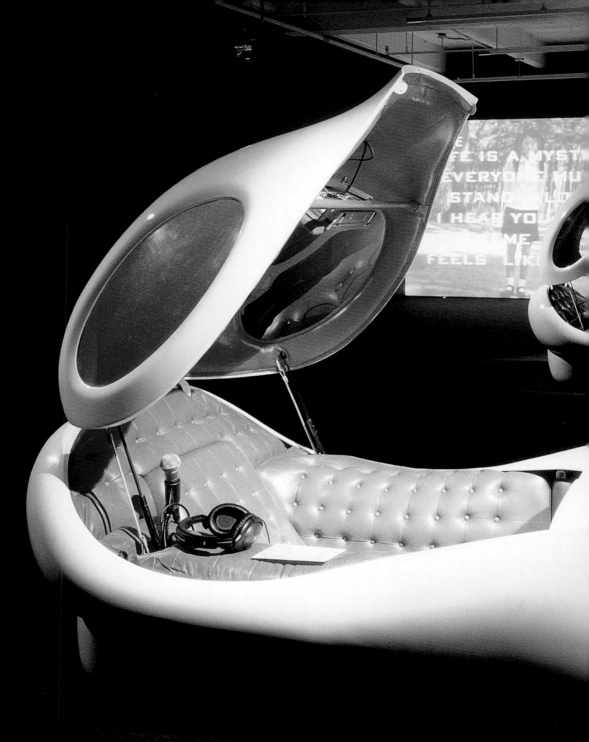

this image and following pages:
Lee Bul: Live Forever, installation
views at The Fabric Workshop
and Museum, 2001
Photo: Will Brown
Video sequence: Matt Suib

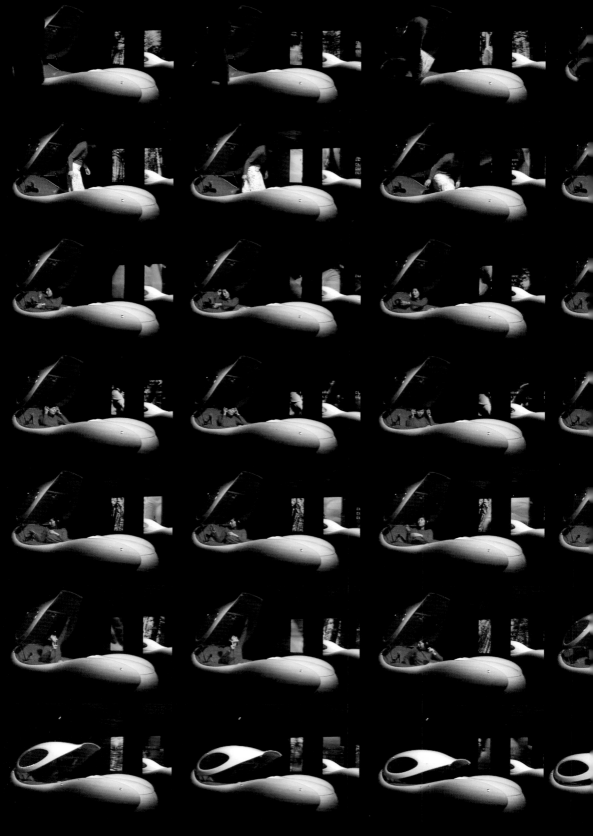

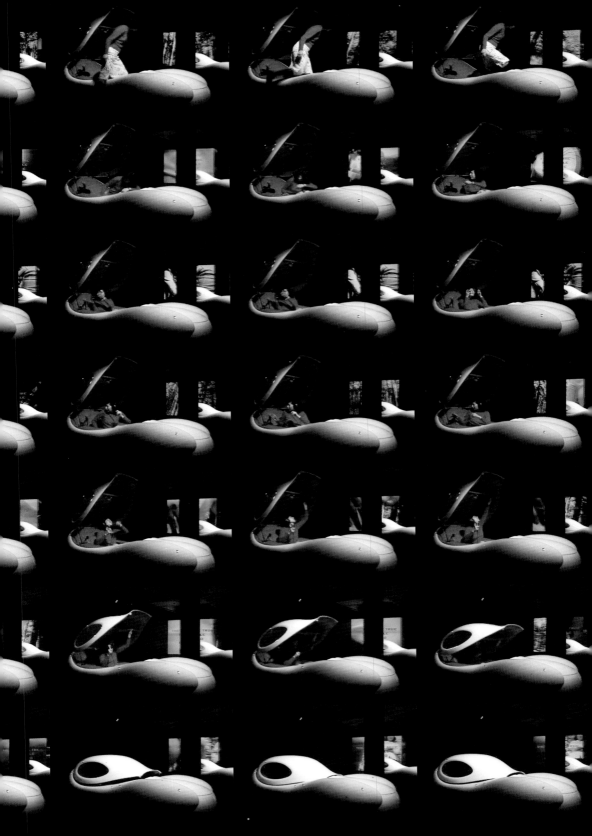

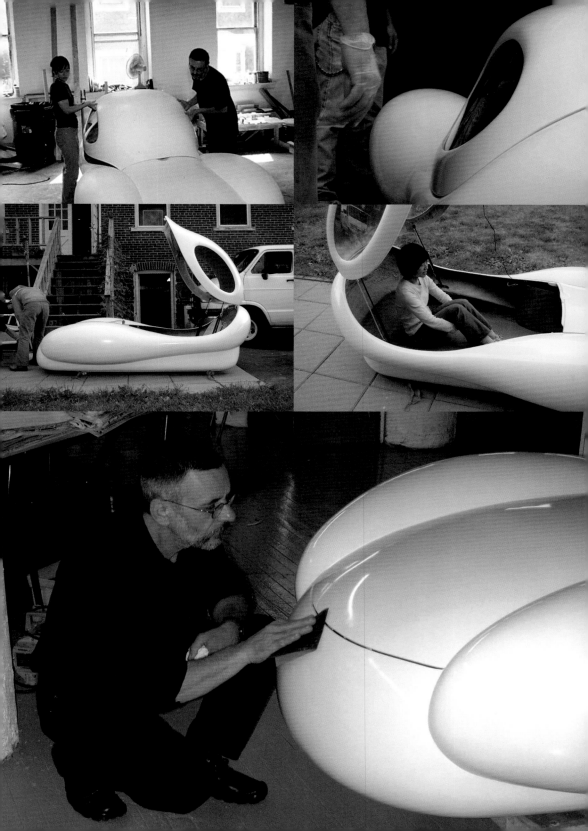

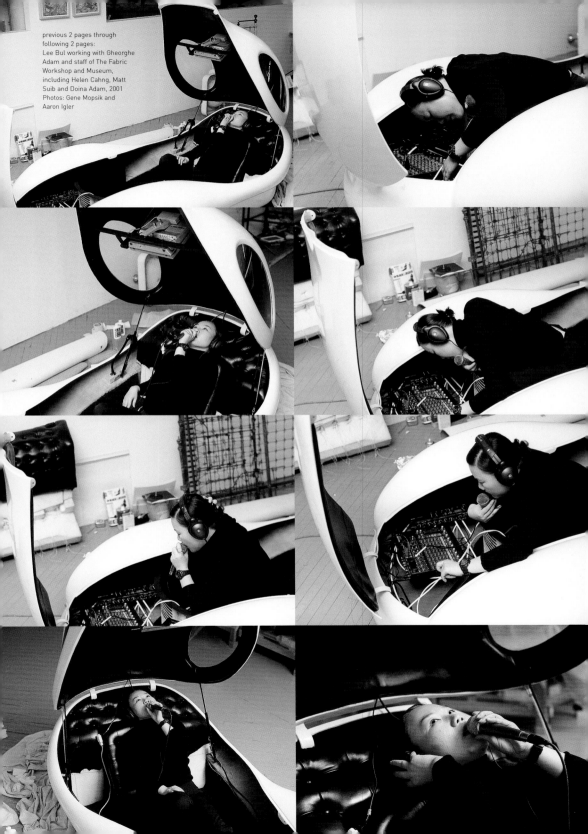

previous 2 pages through
following 2 pages:
Lee Bul working with Gheorghe
Adam and staff of The Fabric
Workshop and Museum,
including Helen Cahng, Matt
Suib and Doina Adam, 2001
Photos: Gene Mopsik and
Aaron Igler

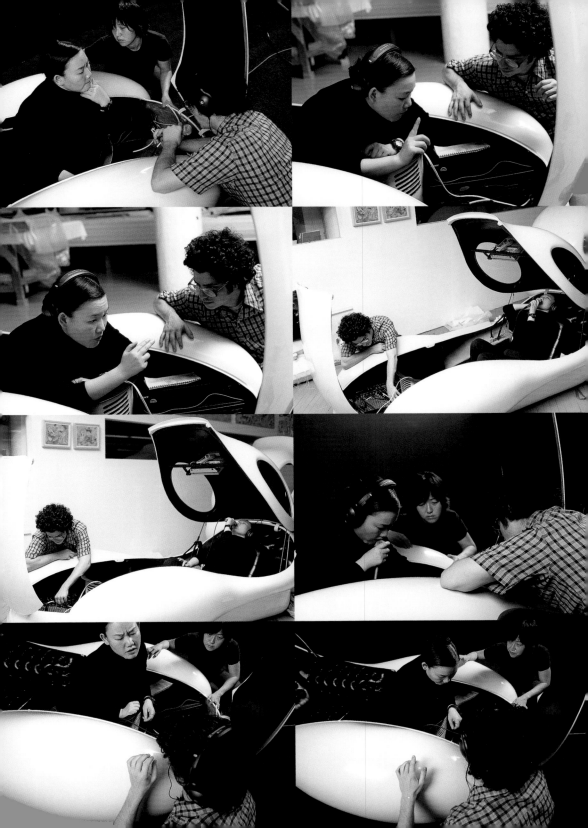

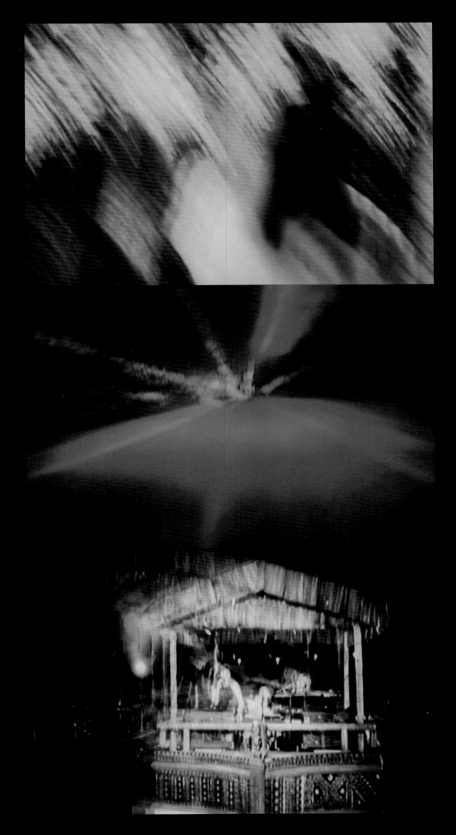

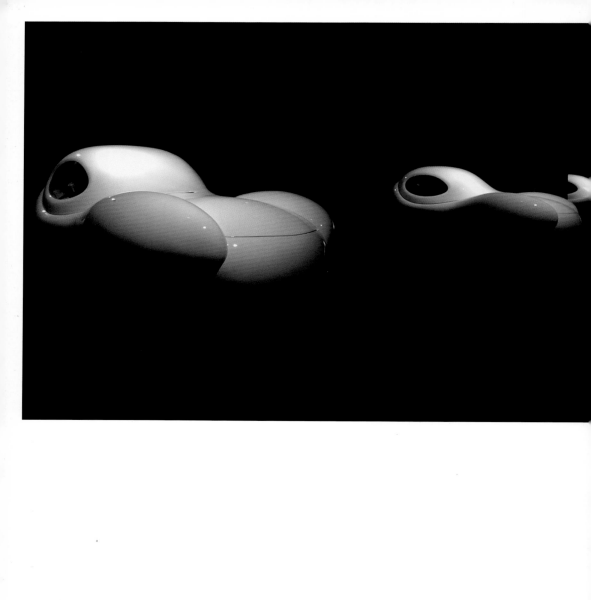

...HEARD OF A VAN
THAT'S LOADED
WITH WEAPONS
PACKED UP AND
READY TO GO

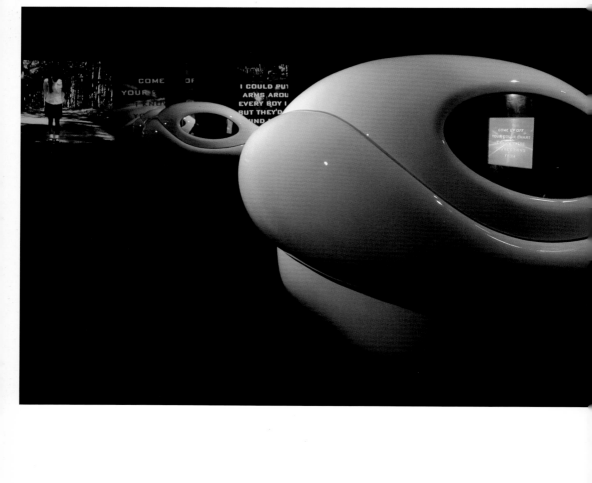

LIKE YOU WERE
WALKING ONTO
A YACHT

THIS AIN'T NO
PARTY
THIS AIN'T NO
DISCO
THIS AIN'T NO
FOOLIN' AROUND

YOU HAD ME
SEVERAL YEARS
AGO WHEN I WAS
STILL QUITE NAIVE

TRANSMIT
THE MESSAGE
TO THE RECEIVER
HOPE FOR AN
ANSWER SOMEDAY

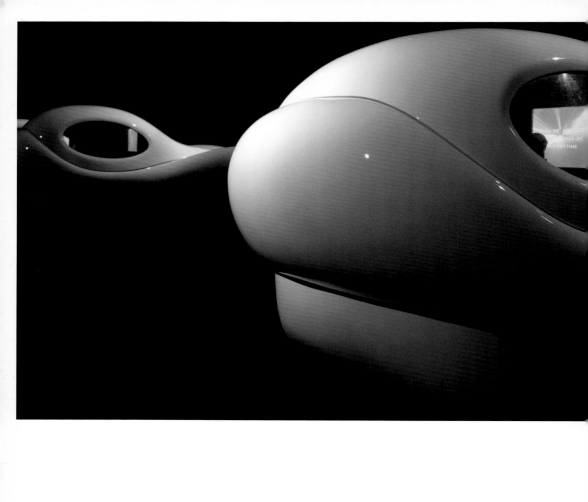

YOU'RE SO VAIN
I BET YOU THINK
THIS SONG IS
ABOUT YOU

BUT I AIN'T GOT
NO SPEAKERS
AIN'T GOT
NO HEADPHONES
AIN'T' GOT NO
RECORDS TO PLAY

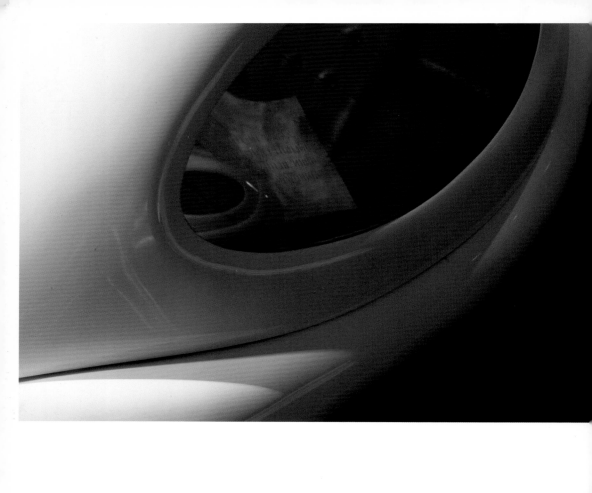

SWEET DREAMS
ARE THE WORLD THIS
WHO AM I
TO DISAGREE

CAN'T WRITE
A LETTER
CAN'T SEND
NO POSTCARD
I CAN'T WRITE
NOTHING AT ALL

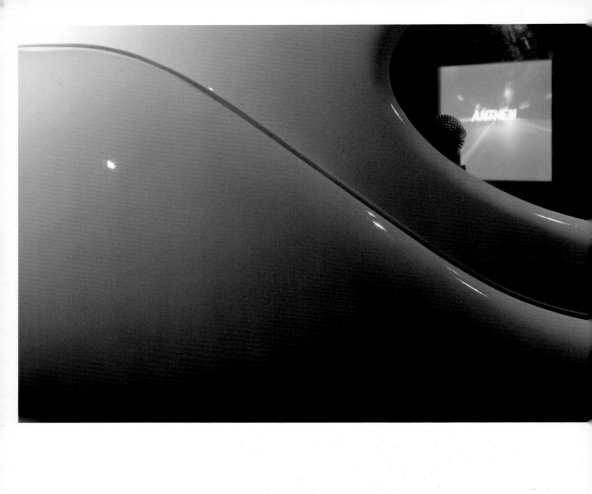

MMM, YEAH, YEAH

The Fabric Workshop and Museum
Staff List

Marion Boulton Stroud, Founder/Artistic Director
Doina Adam, Project Coordinator/Construction Technician
Ursula Ahrens, Assistant Registrar
Tracey Blackman, Museum Shop Manager
Blake Bradford, Education Coordinator
Helen Cahng, Project Coordinator/Construction Technician
Candy Depew, Project Coordinator/Master Printer
Joy Feasley, Preparator
Mary Anne Friel, Project Coordinator/Master Printer
Aaron Igler, Photographer
Virgil Marti, Master Printer
Laurie McGahey, Assistant Director
Ellen Bethany Napier, Associate Director
Sue Patterson, Project Coordinator/Construction Technician
Julie Roat, Bookkeeper
Christina Roberts, Apprentice Training Program Coordinator
Janet Samuel, Registrar
Olivia Schreiner, Studio Assistant
Julie Shelton Snyder, Controller
Matthew Suib, Videographer/Exhibitions Assistant
Paul Swenbeck, Preparator
Kathryn van Voorhees, Administrative Assistant

Kelly Mitchell, Consulting Editor

Ella King Torrey, Marion Stroud, Lee Bul and the staff and Board of the Fabric Workshop and Museum and the San Francisco Art Institute (2002).

The Fabric Workshop and Museum would like to thank its generous funders for their support of this project. The E. Rhodes and Leona B. Carpenter Foundation and the Korea Foundation provided specific support for Lee Bul's residency, exhibition and publication. In addition, we are grateful to the Arcadia Foundation, National Endowment for the Arts, LLWW Foundation, Claniel Foundation, Philip Morris Companies, Miller Plummer Foundation and the Board of Directors and Members of The Fabric Workshop and Museum, who make the residency and exhibition programs possible.

The Fabric Workshop and Museum
1315 Cherry Street, 5th and 6th floors
Philadelphia, PA 19107
Tel 215.568.1111   Fax 215.568.8211
www.fabricworkshopandmuseum.org